A STRATEGY FOR DAILY LIVING

A STRATEGY
FOR DAILY
LIVING

ARI KIEV, M.D.

THE FREE PRESS
A Division of Macmillan Publishing Co., Inc.
NEW YORK

COLLIER MACMILLAN PUBLISHERS
LONDON

Library of Congress Cataloging in Publication Data

Kiev, Ari.
    A strategy for daily living.

    1. Conduct of life.   I. Title.
BJ1581.2.K47   170'.202   73-8092
ISBN 0-02-917160-1

The Free Press
A Division of Macmillan Publishing Co., Inc.
866 Third Avenue, New York, N.Y.   10022

Collier–Macmillan Canada Ltd., Toronto, Ontario

Library of Congress Catalog Card Number: 73-8092

Printed in the United States of America

printing number
    2   3   4   5   6   7   8   9   10

FOR JONATHAN KIEV

The potential in you is new in nature and no one but you can know what you can do, nor will you know until you have tried.

CONTENTS

SEVERAL YEARS AGO a young businessman visited my office with an unusual request. He was in New York City for only a day and was returning that evening to a small town upstate. He wanted a set of guidelines to follow that would let him function without professional help in the face of considerable confusion and despair caused by serious personal problems. "I want some kind of daily checklist to help me keep on track during times of doubt and indecision. I know I must solve my own problems, but if I had some general rules to follow it would make things a lot easier for me," he said.

Intrigued by this challenge I prepared a list of eight principles that were specifically designed to maximize his strengths so that he could cope by himself with his problems. Several months later he phoned to thank me for my help and to tell me that daily he read through the checklist and that it had helped him to resolve many of his most pressing problems. In fact, he had begun to move in new and satisfying directions in his life that in the past he could only allow himself to dream about.

Skeptical of the dramatic benefits resulting from so simple a task as a daily reading of a set of guidelines (which differed from traditional approaches in not focusing on understanding and overcoming weaknesses, or in developing will power through repeated autosuggestions), I began to experiment by giving this daily checklist to various persons as their situations appeared to warrant it. Slowly I expanded the guidelines into a series of daily strategies that were general enough to be applicable to a wide range of human problems and life situations and yet practical enough to help people cope with specific situations, relying on their own specific resources.

Eventually, I organized these strategies into a large mimeographed manuscript and a set of 10 audiocasette messages, which I have given to well over 500 people, who with few exceptions reported that they regularly consulted these guidelines when faced with difficult problems.* Many said that they were led to discover hidden talents and resources and had gained greater satisfaction from their lives. At no time were these strategies intended as a substitute for professional help. Yet they have proved beneficial to people in a variety of emotional and situational crises.

---

*The audiocasette series can be obtained from the Psychodynamic Research Corporation, P.O. Box 1123, Englewood Cliffs, N.J. 07632.

Indeed, I know of no one who has found them harmful, confusing, or in conflict with any of their traditional values.

It is my hope that you, the reader, will find this small book to be of value to you in maximizing your efforts to realize your fondest hopes and aspirations.

Ari Kiev, M.D.

⊸⊰ A WORTHY PURPOSE

At the outset, let me point out that this book does not contain a magical formula for leading your life. Nobody can decide that but you. Nor does it describe what you should do with your life. That, too, is up to you.

What I have set out to do is to describe a day-by-day strategy that will help make each day a more worthwhile one than the day before and will help you to maximize the potential you possess. A successful life does not result from chance nor is it determined by fate or good fortune, but from a succession of successful days. This book will help you plan, rather than merely await, such days.

I have written this book to help you set

the objectives, goals, and styles of life that you want. I'll discuss how you can gain mastery of yourself and develop skills for dealing with obstacles that impede efforts to reach goals. We'll consider how you can identify your strengths, what you can do to prevent the development of upsetting emotions, how to circumvent obstacles, and how to control those habits that create conflict for you in relation to others.

The guidelines for coping I describe in this book must be adapted to your own circumstances. While you will benefit by reading and rereading this book alone, it will prove even more valuable in certain instances if you do it with the guidance of a professional who has been trained to help you to see what you are now doing and what you can do.

In my office practice and in my consultant work with community agencies, religious institutions, and business corporations, I have repeatedly found that helping people to develop personal goals has proved to be the most effective way to help them to cope with problems and maximize their satisfactions.

With goals, people can overcome confusion and conflict over incompatible values, contradictory desires, and frustrated relationships with friends and relatives, all of which often result from the absence of rational life strategies.

Observing the lives of people who have mastered adversity, I have repeatedly noted that they have established goals and, irrespective of obstacles, sought with all their effort to achieve them. From the moment they fixed an objective in their mind and decided to concentrate all their energies on a specific goal, they began to surmount the most difficult odds.

If you acknowledge that your dreams and hopes are worth working for and focus your thoughts on achieving them, your chances of making them a reality will increase.

A powerful dream creates a dynamic force for you. Consider for a moment some of the developments of our time—such as the manned flights to the moon—to recognize that dreams redefined as goals are the fundamental cause of all that has been accomplished by man since the beginning of time. Everything that has been created in the world existed in the thoughts and daydreams of some men before it was realized. This principle has been expressed in the aphorism "what the mind of man can conceive and believe, it can achieve."

The establishment of a goal is the key to successful living. Edward G. Bulwer-Lytton put it this way: "The man who succeeds above his fellows is the one who early in life clearly discerns his object and towards that object he habitually directs his powers. Even genius itself is but fine observation strengthened by fixity of purpose. Every man who observes vigilantly and resolves steadfastly grows unconsciously into genius." Anyone who fixes on a purpose and pursues it can become successful.

Those who lead successful lives have made a disciplined effort to systematically pursue an objective rather than to drift about aimlessly with no objective. "The secret of success," as Disraeli noted, "is constancy to purpose."

Most people describe their goals in terms of vague undefinable conditions of life such as happiness, wealth, and fame.

By goals, I mean specific, concrete objectives that you, as a unique individual, wish to achieve or wish to have. If you can determine what you want, you can determine how to achieve it. Why aren't more people successful? Because most people do not select and pursue a goal without regard for other objectives. Most people shift from one activity to another without any focused or directed purpose, naively assuming that things will take care of themselves or will be taken care of by others.

It's difficult to take charge of your life, decide on goals, and determine how to reach them. I am sure you know what you want and how to lead the "good life." You may even say "I think this is the most important thing to do," "This is what I really like to do," or "If I had my choice, this is what I would do, but I've got to take care of other things first." If you are like most people, you, no doubt, divert your energy in many directions, leaving yourself with little energy, time, or motivation to pursue what you consider most important. If this is true, then you must understand the way you function now, how you can pursue your most important priorities first, and how to avoid distractions that keep you from this.

Many people complain about not knowing what they want to do. It usually turns out that they spend much of their time doing what others want them to do. Because of convention, custom, family tradition, or other obligations, they have not learned to say no to requests for either favors they can ill afford to give or advice they are untrained to give. Nor have they learned to be selective in accepting invitations or commitments that divert energy from more personal interests and objectives.

If this sounds familiar, you need not feel apologetic in justifying your conscientiousness. Once you learn to be selective in saying yes and learn to be comfortable (and not guilty) in saying no, you will have time and energy to determine what you want. At first you may be uncomfortable with your new-found freedom, and may revert to your habit of allowing others to take the responsibility for determining your life. But keep trying. It takes time and practice to develop new habits.

In doing this, try a mixture of self-discipline and imagination with regard to your time. Most people would agree that it makes sense to pay yourself first, to put some money in the bank before you start paying out your bills. You've got to conserve your own time the same way. Give time to your special areas of interest. Then you will have free time and can give it to others in the ways in which you decide. People won't impose on you as much once you have learned to take care of your own needs first, since there will be times when you must say no. They will be reluctant to impose their requests once they discover that you're not a "doormat."

I am sure you have at least thirty minutes each day to list all your thoughts about possible goals. Try for ten ideas each day. In thirty days you'll have 300 ideas from which to select one or more objectives on which to set your mind.

It's important not to delay. Begin this exercise at once. While the thought is fresh in your mind, get a pencil and paper and write down five goals you wish to attain. Develop this habit of writing such thoughts down whenever you have them. Later on, add them to your list of possible goals. In the same way that a foundation must be laid before a building can be built or a course set before a ship can reach its destination, the final goal must be incorporated into the first act.

Indeed, the most important step in achieving a goal is to define the goal. It only takes one outstanding idea to lead to your first fortune, to revolutionize the character of your life, or to change the nature of your work.

If you have not yet decided on one thing you want more than anything else in the world, take some time to prepare a list of the things you want. Such things might include a trip to Bermuda, a specific amount of money in the bank, a particular kind of job. After writing them all down, choose the most important and record it separately on a single card. Put the master list aside, returning to it only after you have achieved the first objective.

Carry this card with you at all times. Think about this objective every day. Create concrete mental images of the goal, as if you've already accomplished it. This will make it a living reality for you. The more you keep your goal in the forefront of your mind, the more likely you will be to come up with ways to achieve it.

Check the card each day, in this way building a positive expectancy about its completion. This will assure success. You are what you think about. Setting your mind to a goal and concentrating on its achievement will bring a renewed vigor, purpose, and sense of vitality to your life.

If your objective is to obtain a certain house, draw up a picture of it. If your objective is to earn a specific income, write down the amount. Believing in it, deciding on it, you will achieve it.

Similarly, the more you believe that you will not succeed, the more likely you are to fail. Negative expectations result in failures, since they initiate the self-fulfilling prophecy. As long as you set up an expectation, you are likely to realize that expectation, to the extent that we become what we think about. Take time out each day to plan your goals for the next day. What do you hope to accomplish? A succession of daily goals may suggest a long-range goal to you.

Once actively engaged in activity that interests you, you will find much to do and will develop an awareness of new capacities in yourself. Goal-directed activity should develop from positive assets. To the extent that you begin to define yourself by your actions in areas of your greatest strengths, you will develop a new sense of yourself.

As Spinoza said, "To be what we are and to become what we are capable of becoming, is the only end to life." The more involved you become in activity, the more satisfied and self-realized you will be.

A goal will clarify your sense of identity. It will give you a standard against which to judge opportunities and choices. It will help you to pick the most important matters from a mass of information input and to strengthen your ability to say no to less important commitments.

You can reach only one goal at a time. Uncertainty, doubt, and indecision occur when you have not settled on a single objective and accomplish little because you shift from one thing to another.

Don't be afraid of failure. As Herodotus wrote, "It is better by noble boldness to run the risk of being subject to half of the evils we anticipate than to remain in cowardly listlessness for fear of what may happen."

⚜ YOUR HIDDEN POTENTIAL

MANY PEOPLE ARE dissatisfied, even though they have what they believe everyone wants and should want—a nice home, a good job, and the like. They are unfulfilled by their achievements or acquisitions and even their relationships. But they don't know why they are uncomfortable or what it is they really want. Assessing their lives, they will likely discover how little effort they devote to what they really want to do.

What leads to this misplaced effort, to this lack of meaningful direction? Many difficulties result from faulty self-images learned in your earliest years. Much of your personality and your concept about yourself comes from the emphasis on and the neglect of

--⚜ 14 ⚜--

different features of your personality during your childhood. If this emphasis matched your temperament, talents, and special skills, you have developed an accurate and realistic self-image. If not, you have probably experienced much conflict. You may, for example, have an inclination to paint, but may have been conditioned to reject this or you may have even developed a revulsion toward painting. The more you become aware of these suppressed sides of yourself, the more you will be able to accept and utilize hidden potential. While your choices as a child may have been limited, they need no longer be limited. You decide what you do with your life. In the last analysis, your behavior, not chance or the concepts of others, determines your concept of yourself and determines whether or not you will reach the goals you set.

The requirements of society, which ask people to conform to certain norms, tend to submerge the uniqueness of individuals, especially in their early years. Early training conditions many habits that may operate to excess when people are older—habits of depending on others, checking with others, restraining one's self-assertiveness.

Unfortunately, the world that you were prepared for as a child is not the same as the world you live in as an adult. But the limitations you impose upon yourself derive less from the nature of the world than from incorrect concepts you have learned in childhood. To be true to your inner nature, you've got to become free of these cultural distortions which, though they may have made you feel comfortable, have at the same time limited you. As you correct your distorted perceptions of the world and accept responsibility for your life, you will see the world more realistically. Richard L. Evans said, "May we never let the things we can't have or don't have or shouldn't have spoil our enjoyment of the things we do have and can have. As we value our happiness, let us not forget it. One of the greatest lessons in life is learning to be happy without the things we cannot or should not have."

Your parents and teachers may have mistakenly ignored your strengths or may not have encouraged you to develop them. Parents impose their own limited concepts on their children, often ignoring their temperament, special needs, and abilities. You can discover your basic capacities by experimenting with things that you always wanted to do. Don't be discouraged by notions that seem "silly" or "foolish" or "not you." Do it! Who knows what will happen?

In some cultures, one can have two jobs. In others, this is unacceptable, and free time must be given to community or charity work, not what interests you. If you are a woman, you may have been discouraged from engaging in business or pursuing a career. Pursuing such objectives, you may anticipate opposition. Don't expect encouragement from others who may find it difficult to conceive of how you might be any way other than the way you are. If you follow your inclination to pursue your objectives, you will discover that others—your husband or wife, your parents, and your friends—will respect you even more.

Focus on strengths, not on weaknesses. Focus on what you can do. Build your resources. Focus on the aspects of your daily life that you take for granted. You have more potential than you may think. Consider how much your mental energies have accomplished for you until now. Your job, what you earn, your accomplishments to date have generally come from the application of your intelligence to various tasks around you. Like most people, you probably use only a portion of your mental powers. If all your accomplishments have resulted from using only a portion of your capabilities, consider how much you can accomplish if you tap your hidden potential.

Setting up challenges for yourself by establishing goals will bring some of this potential to the surface.

Booker T. Washington said, "I have learned that success is to be measured not so much by the position that one has reached in life as by the obstacles that he has overcome while trying to succeed." For many, life has become too comfortable and easy, and not challenging enough to spur them to positive action.

Tryon Edwards said, "There is nothing so elastic as the human mind; like imprisoned steam, the more it is pressed, the more it rises to resist the pressure. The more we are obliged to do, the more we are able to accomplish."

Encountering obstacles, you will increase the range of resources that you bring into play. What is it that you spend so much of your time on that diminishes the application of your intellect to the problems around you? For one thing, you probably spend a great deal of time worrying about things that have never happened, or about things that happened but that can't be changed or solved personally. You probably spend the least amount of time worrying about important matters or solving problems related to your objectives.

You need only examine your present situation to discover unlimited resources and opportunities. It is not necessary to search elsewhere.

Before you begin to give up what you have in favor of something that looks more desirable from a distance, examine what you do have, because if you don't, someone else will.

Ruskin put it this way: "The weakest among us has a gift, however seemingly trivial, which is peculiar to him and which worthily used will be a gift also to his face." The real trick is not in acquiring a greater fortune, more prestige, or more power, but in finding out your gift and putting it to use. What's special about you? What is that unique combination of traits and attitudes and abilities you have that never before in history has appeared on the face of the earth? You won't find this gift outside of yourself, but in your own activities. What can you comfortably do? What do you like to do? What do you do well? What do others think you do well? What do you do automatically? What kinds of things do you do naturally in your spare time? Stop and think. Are you using your intelligence and your energies to their greatest capacity? You probably use only a fraction of your abilities and you probably don't use to maximum advantage other resources you already possess. Your books contain a wealth of ideas; your telephone links you in communication with the entire world; your radio is a constant source of information; your typewriter is a machine for producing legible documents. Through correspondence you can attend a university without leaving your room. One hundred years ago, the richest men in the world depended on many people to receive and transmit equivalent amounts of information. You may be ignoring what's at your fingertips. Think of it this way. If you sleep eight hours and work eight hours each day, you still have more than seventy hours of free time each week left to pursue your objectives. That equals 3,640 hours a year.

As Francis Bacon wrote, "A wise man will make more opportunites than he finds." You can prepare for situations that will occur for the very reason that you have prepared for them.

Edwin Huble Chapin put it this way: "The best men, not those who have waited for chances, but who have taken them; be-seiged the chance; conquered the chance; and made chance the servator."

Opportunities abound around us, and it is up to the individual to take advantage of these opportunities. As Kipling wrote at the end of his famous poem"If," "If you can fill the unforgiving minute with sixty seconds worth of distance run, yours is the earth and everything that's in it."

Samuel Johnson put it differently: "To improve the golden moment of opportunity and catch the good that is within our reach, is the great art of life."

Montaigne said, "The great and glorious masterpiece of men is to live to the point. All other things—to reign [lord it over others], to hoard, to build—are at most but in considerable props and appendages." Your gift may be that which you do best and most readily. You should work to improve it. Others may discourage you from pursuing this, advising conformity instead. Don't allow yourself to be influenced. You need not feel guilty about doing those things at which you are successful, even though what others recommend may appear to be more important or acceptable. Following such advice may only lead you away from activity in the very areas of interest where you will maximize your sense of accomplishment and satisfaction. You must make an effort to rediscover the aspects of your basic nature that may have been submerged beneath the surface during your early years. At some point, you have to take yourself as you are; you must recognize that you are equipped to contribute in some special way to the world, that you should not passively act in a way that is determined by others.

You can determine your special talents or strengths in a number of ways, ranging from psychological tests to an analysis of the unexpressed wishes in your dreams. Remember, no one method works for everyone. You might start, for example, by clipping and pasting newspaper articles that interest you for the next thirty days. At the end of that time, see if there isn't some trend suggestive of a deep-seated interest or natural inclination. Keep alert each day to the slightest indications of special skills or talents, even when they seem silly or unimportant to you. Take note of the remarks of friends and relatives when they say that something is "typical of you." Perhaps as a child you had certain leanings that you never developed. Consider these, as well.

From this exercise, you should be able to get some sense of potential strengths. Whenever you discover a strength or talent, think of five possible ways to develop this strength. Write these down on a 3×5 inch card and check them periodically to keep them fresh in your mind. You need go no further than where you are now standing to harness your strengths; and when you do, you will be amazed at how much inner satisfaction you will create for yourself. Remember, you have been building this basic strength all your life, although you may not have been utilizing it.

Perhaps your parents set you on the right track, encouraged you to study and to pursue a particular career. That's fine. How you do it and when you do it and, in fact, whether you do it at all, however, ought to be determined by you and no one else. Begin to reassess all that you do to meet the expectations and obligations set for you by others. Perhaps some of these things are not compatible with your temperament. Are you inclined to be meticulous and exacting, to want everything to add up to the third decimal point? Great— that's terrific if you are an accountant, a nuclear physicist, or a structural engineer; but I'm not so sure that the same traits will help in cleaning a house or selling radios and televisions. Each of us has inherited a different temperament. If you are an intuitive, artistic, and creative person, you'll be frustrated if you work in accounting. Similarly, if you like an ordered and structured world, you probably don't belong in a carnival-type atmosphere or in ambiguous situations. Different situations fit different temperaments. Familiarize yourself with your tendencies in order to size up a situation in advance, so that you can determine whether it is "your cup of tea." Avoid situations which upset you. If you feel compelled to drink at a cocktail party or in high-pressure social situations to feel comfortable, you are probably too anxious and would do better to avoid such situations.

⊶ GOAL SELECTION

EFFORT DIRECTED toward a meaningful goal facilitates the realization of human potential.

If you accept the proposition that the situation you find yourself in now results from your concept of yourself, then you should be willing to test the proposition that your present situation will change in the direction that you want it to as you gain control over your thoughts and attitudes. As you concentrate on your goals and ignore thoughts of failure, self-doubt, worry, anxiety, or less important matters, you will reach your objectives.

You control the direction of your life. Only your self-concept limits you from achieving your fullest capacity. Since changes in behavior generally precede changes in attitude, action directed towards your goals will increase your sense of purpose and belief in the possibility of success.

How can you develop a self-concept linked to your untapped potential? First, you can decide on the kind of life you would like to lead in ten or fifteen years. This will give you a standard for making decisions about current activities and will reduce the inclination to compare yourself unfavorably to others. Learn to ask, "How would I handle this situation were I the person I hope to become?" If an activity has no relationship to your objectives, don't do it.

Would the person that you want to be take on those extra tasks, drive a particular automobile, engage in particular business practices? Setting an objective will minimize your indecision in making choices about matters unrelated to your goals.

Many people promise themselves that

some day they are going to "let go" and "do what they want to do." Unfortunately, the day never comes. Only when circumstances push them or when they "have nothing to lose" do they do what they have always wanted to do.

Without a central goal, your thoughts may become worrisome; your confidence and morale may be undermined and you may be led to the feared circumstances. Without a goal, you will focus on your weaknesses and the possibilities of error and criticism. This will foster indecision, procrastination, and inadequacy, and will impede the development of your potential.

The mature person assumes responsibility for what happens to him and does not attribute misfortune to the environment or the failure of others. He learns from experience by asking "What else could I have done?" He realizes that he can change no one but himself.

To reach your objectives, you must rise above the motivation to satisfy only physical needs and desires. Large goals require greater commitment and the postponement of present gratification for future reward. The greater the task, the more you must assume responsibility for managing yourself.

Don't focus on past failures or exaggerated fears of future failures. This can distract you from the here and now. "I have never done this," "So and so won't like this," and "We usually don't do it this way," are rationalizations for the failure to act. Similarly, a crisis may provide justification for inaction, when actually a crisis can provide the chance to reassess and improve your strategies for living.

Action will give you a sense of identity, will reduce conflict and inhibition, and will increase your capacity to make your own choices. Pursuit of your objectives in your own way creates a sense of freedom. Look for the greatest opportunity for change in the areas that you take for granted. Handle simple choices first, difficult ones last. (The more you deal with simple decisions, the easier your life will become.) Choice is more difficult in interpersonal relationships, marriage, divorce, and job location. Before changing these radically, consider what you can do in the situation you are now in that gives you the most opportunity to express yourself. Then explore ways in which you can increase your effort in these areas.

How many goals should you have? One goal should be sufficient. Too many goals, conflicting goals, or impossible goals produce conflict. A single goal will simplify your life, help you to define an identity, conserve energy, and reduce dependency on others.

Uncertainty about your goals fosters a tendency to lean unnecessarily on others, as if they were experts. This may lead to uncertainty and ambivalence and discourage positive action. Neither the "experts," adversity, or public opinion should deter you from your goals.

Focus on one objective at a time. Like a servomechanism, the brain, set on a target, will call into play those mental processes that will bring your efforts to fruition. In line with the self-fulfilling prophecy, your actions will conform to your expectations, thereby bringing about the event. If you believe that you will reach your objective, you will continue to work at a task until you have accomplished it and will not give up because of the uncertainty of the result.

How can you keep on target all the time? First, you can think through the steps you will take along the way to achieving your goal—practicing, so to speak, with your imagination. Since the mind can think of only one thing at a time, this practice planning will reinforce your involvement in your efforts. You can facilitate your daily planning by listing on a small 3 × 5 inch card your major objective, and the three immediate steps you plan to take to reach it. Checking this card each day will enable you to visualize your objective and to review the relationship between what you have done each day and your objective. If this suits your temperament, it can be very valuable. If it doesn't you'll have to find some other way in which to keep on your track.

Always have the next goal in the back of your mind, since the most satisfaction comes from the process of pursuing a goal, not simply from achieving it.

Above all, don't be impatient about reeaching your objectives. Harold V. Melchert put it this way: "Live your life each day as you would climb mountains. An occasional glance towards the summit puts the goal in mind. Many beautiful scenes can be observed from each new vantage point. Climb steadily, slowly, enjoy each passing moment; and the view from the summit will serve as a fitting climax to the journey."

Everyone wants to be rewarded for his efforts. Don't, as many do, delay in making the effort until you are assured of a reward. Have faith that your rewards will follow your efforts, in accordance with the law of cause and effect. If you try to obtain the rewards without making the effort to earn them, you will find frustration and failure and will be denied the satisfaction of a job well done.

An excessive concern for rewards creates fear about making the effort and leads to failure.

⚜ STEP-BY-STEP PLANNING

THE MODERN WORLD makes innumerable demands on an individual's time and resources. This creates conflicts and psychological stress. Despite limited time, you may overcommit yourself, leaving little time for your most important activities. You may belong to various groups and organizations that expect you to devote some of your time to committee work or meetings. You may feel that you must attend a wedding, a cocktail party, a business luncheon, or a community meeting. You may wish you could spend more time on evenings and weekends with your family. You may be plagued by failures in the past, by what you did wrong, or by what you've done against your better judgment. To resolve these conflicting demands, you must learn to regulate your time.

Every activity that consumes time in the present must be assessed in terms of your priorities. If you are in business, this activity may be your most productive account. If you are a research worker, your project may be most important and challenging priority. If you are a housewife, it may be raising your children. To accomplish your objective, you must develop the habit of doing first things first.

Having set your goal, focus on what you can do each day and keep at it. Deal with the here and now. You need only concentrate on the efforts you make. The results will take care of themselves. Excessive preoccupation with the future may lead you to exaggerate difficulties and to try anxiously to bring about results in ways other than through the maximum utilization of your talents.

Remember these words of Seneca: "If we

do not watch, we lose our opportunities; if we do not make haste, we are left behind; our best hours escape us, the worst are to come, the purest part of our life runs first and leaves only the dregs at the bottom, in that time which is good for nothing else, we dedicate to virtue and only propose to begin to live at an age that very few people arrive at."

To maximize the moment, you must prepare for it. To achieve your goals, you must prepare yourself so that you will actually create the opportunities you wish to find.

Remember that opportunities can't always be recognized. Iron ore in no way resembles iron or steel. Only if you prepare will you recognize opportunities.

How can you prepare? Take your job as a starting point. Are you knowledgeable in all phases of your work? Do you know the origins of your industry? What new developments will occur in your field in the next ten years? The more you learn about your field, the more capable you'll be in recognizing opportunities as they appear.

Rather than settling down in your work at some plateau, assuming that you are likely to continue to function at that particular job until pension time, begin to look for ways in which you can grow within your own setting, ways in which you can become more valuable in your job or in your community or at home.

Don't be afraid to take risks. These need not be skydiving and mountain climbing, but simply active efforts in simple daily activities that are so often avoided because of the demands of courtesy, social obligation, or the need to act according to the expectations that others have of you. Make a list of ten steps you would take if you were the person you would like to become. Take that course that you have been thinking about; invest in what you have been thinking about; try a new venture; try a new route to work; try taking a subway if you have been taking a bus; try taking a bus if you have been taking your car.

Delay leads to more delay. Inertia, not lack of information, fosters indecision. Postponement can become habitual and can lead to nonproductivity. It may mean acommodation and revision of programs and schedules, but you must recognize that when you postpone your involvement in something, you will probably never accomplish it, and will be left with memories of past wishes rather than of past deeds.

Bypass obstacles by initiating alternative activities. This reduces conflict and frustration and permits you to continue the pursuit of your goal. Focusing on grievances intensifies their significance and magnifies fears and worries.

Must you be consistent? Must you stick to your original plans? No. As Emerson wrote, "A foolish consistency is the hobgoblin of little minds adored by little statesmen and philosophers and divines." Generally, most of us remember only this portion of Emerson's quote. The rest is equally helpful. "With consistency a great soul has simply nothing to do. He may as well concern himself with his shadow on the wall. Speak what you think now in hard words and tomorrow speak what tomorrow thinks in hard words again, though it contradict everything you said to-day.— 'Ah, so you shall be sure to be misunderstood.' " Is it so bad then to be misunderstood? Pythagoras was misunderstood, and Socrates, and Jesus, and Luther, and Copernicus, and Galileo, and Newton, and every pure and wise spirit that ever took flesh. To be great is to be misunderstood."

As you begin each day, you have the freedom to try new approaches. There is no reason to think that you even have to stay on the same job or live in the same house. The more you discover and master the freedom you have, the more you will determine your own destiny. This does not mean you should rush from one situation to another willy-nilly or escape responsibility by making drastic or extreme changes. Freedom is not license, nor should you become the servant or slave of your own impulses. You, not the situation, can and should change.

Stop and think what you can change in the smallest areas of your daily life. If you have been wearing black shoes, try brown ones; if you have been wearing striped ties, try dotted ones; if you have been wearing dull, conservative suits, try a sports jacket; try a different hair style; try different routes. Try something new at your job. Innovate. Such small changes will generate challenge and excitement, will demonstrate the impact you can have over your own destiny, and will spur you on toward fulfilling your objectives.

Daily goals that can be achieved will help you to focus on the present. A simple guideline for accomplishing this would be to spend several minutes each night planning for the next day's activities, and only those activities that you can actually engage in. Schedule your time in terms of these activities. The plan will enable you to get going right away the next day and the time schedule will help you in conserving time for yourself. James Russell Lowell once said: "No man is born into the world whose work is not born with him. There is always work and tools to work with for those who will, and blessed are the horny hands of toil. The busy world shoves angrily aside the man whose hands are idle until occasion tells him what to do; and he who waits to have his task marked out shall die and leave his errand unfulfilled."

Focus on what you can do with what you have at hand. Do one thing at a time. Don't get flustered and confused by trying to do several things at once. Too many activities will inundate you and create a feeling of failure. Sit down and write out the three most important tasks you want to accomplish tomorrow. Focus all the effort you can on the essentials of each task. Start with the first, then move on to the next. It may be that at first you can only devote one hour a day to the activity that really matters to you. But even one hour a day can really add up. One hour a day will mean seven hours a week, 365 hours a year, and 3,650 hours in ten years. You can accomplish much in that period of time, taking a course, writing a book, painting a portrait. You certainly have one hour a day even if you divide it into six ten-minute periods. What can you do with ten minutes? In ten minutes you can do some exercises and get your circulation moving again; you can write a letter to a friend; make three phone calls; get out some bills or play a quick game of handball.

Measuring time spent in various activities will help you to determine how much you are focusing on your highest priorities.

For one week, record the amount of time you spend chatting on the telephone. Also note with whom and about what you talk. This can illuminate how much time you spend profitably and how much you waste in idle conversation. You may be spending time with others against your better judgment because of feelings of obligation or as an excuse for not using your time to satisfy your own personal needs and desires.

You may feel that people are blocking you from doing what you want to do. Most people want to keep things the same. In this modern world, where everything is changing so rapidly, people make conscious efforts to sustain the familiar and continue with the past. As such, any change in the directions you take may evoke anxiety in others who find it hard to adjust to your new ways, which may not fit their concept of you. Don't be deterred by this. In fact, when people start questioning you about your new attitudes, take it as a clue that you have begun to move in the new direction you have set for yourself.

You may say, "What does this all have to do with depression?" Stop and think. What has given you difficulty? Most unlikely, the common denominator is failure to strive for a worthy objective and failure to become involved in activities compatible with your temperament and your talents and, as a result, failure to gain the sense of self-realization that comes from the expression of these talents. Here, too, don't allow preconceived notions of what you can accomplish govern your behavior. Don't decide beforehand that you won't be able to accomplish something or that you won't be allowed to do it. Try and try again. With persistence you can accomplish almost anything you set your mind to accomplish. Even Babe Ruth struck out

1,330 times. The man who hasn't made mistakes hasn't been involved in what he's been doing. Don't worry about the errors.

To ensure success, divide your activity into stages and focus on the most important steps and on those most likely to produce first results by the end of the day. Immediate results when you first begin a task will reinforce your confidence and enable you to sustain even greater and longer periods of continued activity without results.

A common error is to shun activity to avoid error or to withdraw from complicated tasks before completing them. Redefine the activity. Divide it up into its component parts. Start doing what you can do now! You can modify your course of action more readily when you are in motion than when you are standing still.

If you lack a sense of achievement from involvement in too many activities, reduce the number. Set objectives which can be achieved each day as well as over longer periods of time.

The more you break tasks down to their elementary components, particularly to those which you are in fact able to do, the more readily you will be able to accomplish the more difficult and complicated tasks. Above all, you must overcome the inclination to minimize the significance of the things you do readily, concentrating on those things that you have difficulty doing and that continue to reinforce your negative image of yourself. What you do well is certainly worthwhile; the more you can strengthen this, the more capable and satisfied you will become, thereby reducing the significance of your weaknesses. The belief that you can't do something is merely a rationalization for unwillingness to take a risk.

Proceed step by step. If you want, you can fly a jet plane. If you can't fly now, you can take lessons and build up training, experience, and flying hours, and advance from a Piper Cub to a Lear Jet. You may, of course, encounter physical limitations or age requirements. Fine, but take it as far as you can. Don't say, "Well, that's not for me, even though I'd like to do it." If you'd like to do it, you can do it if you follow the necessary steps.

According to Ernest Newman, the English music critic, "The greatest composer does not sit down to work because he is inspired, but becomes inspired because he is working. Beethoven, Wagner, Bach, and Mozart settled down day after day to the job in hand with as much regularity as an accountant settles down each day to his figures. They didn't waste time waiting for inspiration." An overriding goal governed the activities of these composers and others, enabling them to overcome the most extreme handicaps. Activity itself generates the impetus for further activity.

MODIFICATION OF BEHAVIOR

WHEN AWAKE, thoughts are continually being generated by the very nature of brain activity. In crisis your brain will automatically respond to the diversity, multiplicity, frequency, and rapidity of new information that it has processed. How you will react will depend on how you have been trained to handle the information and how you have been programmed in the past. You can master a complex crisis if you can identify the important information, refrain from acting impulsively, and if you do not respond to the anxiety triggered in you by the crisis. If you cannot do this, you will be governed by your own untrained emotional impulses, which overwhelm your consciousness and impair your potential to respond intelligently.

You can train yourself to master the stress of crises. To do this, you must first recognize and then bypass all those thoughts grounded in superstition, myth, customs, and convention, which color your responses and attitudes and prevent you from assessing each crisis as a new situation with its own special features. You must train yourself to examine the facts, to assess reality, and to correct for the distortions you introduce by virture of habit. A good example of this is the prejudice toward anything new or strange or unfamiliar. By adopting a scientific attitude, you open up opportunities for yourself to discover much that is good and beautiful in the world around you. By adopting, at the very least, a "wait and see" attitude to new situations and anticipated events, you eliminate the chances of initiating a self-cycling pattern of anxiety and you increase the chances for your own personal growth.

How you think will influence the external characteristics of your life experience. What you adapt to will reflect what you want to adapt to. What you plan to achieve will be mirrored in what you do achieve, in accordance with the self-fulfilling prophesy that people tend to act to bring about that which they perceive to already exist.

The stressfulness of a situation depends on your conception of it. If you view it as a challenge and act accordingly, you will master it and strengthen your capacity to master subsequent stresses. If you view it as disastrous, you will succumb to apathy and fatalism and will fail to take those extra steps within your power to master the situation. The aborigine victim of bone pointing or Voodoo death has accepted the verdict of the witch doctor's bones and has given up hope.

Once you discover that you can govern

your own thinking and that in doing so you can overcome adversity, you will have gained the self-mastery that is inherent in all of us.

Careful preparation improves the capacity to endure hardship and stress. Individuals gain strength in direct proportion to their knowledge of the stresses and their familiarity with their own characteristic responses to stress. The more you understand how you reacted in the past, the better you can anticipate your reactions in the future. Knowing these reactions will help you to control them and to cope with the most severe stresses. This, of course, takes time; at first you catch yourself repeating old habits. Eventually you can anticipate and control them.

How successfully you behave throughout the duration of a crisis will always reflect how well you have developed habits of self-reliance and personal autonomy.

To the extent that you can govern your thoughts, you can master all situations or circumstances in which you find yourself, since you have the capacity to grow and evolve toward the goals you select.

When was the last time you applied your intellect to a new project designed to elevate your self-concept by overcoming habitual patterns of thought? Probably not since school, when you were required to master complex material, which seemed impossible until you began to apply yourself with dedication.

Few people receive real training in the conscious application of thought to problems or tasks. Only from efforts in this direction can you begin to realize the power within you. Rarely will you develop new strengths, without some evidence that these had lain dormant within you. You should learn to search your past to discover these strengths.

You may soon discover that often you act not from an inner impulse, but from a desire to behave according to how others expect you to behave. Simple everyday examples of this occur all the time—when you catch yourself smiling or agreeing with opinions which privately you detest, when you reluctantly share personal matters with others simply because they have pressed you for an answer, or when you willingly agree to some social activity simply because you have little to do and wish to avoid the discomfort of saying no.

When you find yourself behaving in these ways, you will realize how much the events of your day and of your life are governed by your own decisions and resulting behavior. A simple experiment will prove this to you. Try responding differently in one such everyday situation; observe how the simple decision to say no instead of yes, or to refrain from agreeing with something you condemn, significantly alters the ensuing experiences. Once you have seen this, you will be convinced of the impact of your own decisions upon your experience and ultimately upon your environment. You may in fact be able to alter unfavorable circumstances, by modifying your own thoughts, attitudes, and decisions.

Observing yourself will help you gain control over your thoughts and actions. In the last analysis, self-control provides the key to the mastery of stress. The more you attempt to observe your actions and the more you can recognize the influence of your own decisions on these actions, the greater will be your capacity to consider alternative courses of action in every situation you encounter. You will not be pulled continually by the weight of custom, habit, or the social pressure to conform.

You can learn to apply this skill of self-observation wherever and whenever you wish, and can learn to concentrate and to relax simultaneously, so that you can, without experiencing tension or anxiety, concentrate your thoughts on the task or problem at hand

and be confident that the outcome of your actions will be commensurate with your effort.

If you are like most people, you may be reluctant to direct your life in this way, to develop a life plan that will maximize your success or comfort. You may be reluctant to plan ahead in a situation or in a relationship —as if this were manipulative or dishonest and lacked spontaneity. Even though you know what you have done before, you may be reluctant to think through what you would prefer to do in the future—as if you must take as given what happens to you and must refrain from efforts to control your reactions and ultimately your own destiny.

Why is this so? Fear of change; fear of the reactions of others when you do the unexpected; fear that others will be shocked or hurt or angry if you act differently from what they expect of you. This guidebook has been designed to assist you to be more aware of such tendencies so that you can live each day of your life in a more rational way, capitalizing on your past experiences and your ability to assess the situations that you encounter.

The most effective way to deal with fear or anxiety is through the acquisition of information and through focusing activity. If you implement what you have learned, you will demonstrate to yourself and to others that you are not overwhelmed by fear. Study of a task and effort testing it lead to knowledge. Failure as a result of effort yields information that can be applied the next time. The same principle pertains to criticism that, however unpleasant, can provide valuable information about ways to improve. Don't dwell on potential sources of difficulty beyond the limited amount of information available to you. Lack of information will only magnify your illusions of fear and anxiety.

To overcome fear of failure, analyze the

steps you must take to accomplish a task. This analysis may clarify for you the skills you must acquire and may help you to devise a rational plan of action. Facts and skills will dispel fear. Every effort you make should be designed to provide you with more information, which will facilitate your efforts the next time. Rodin said that "nothing is a waste of time if you use the experience wisely." Even unrewarding, unsatisfying, and unsatisfactory experience can be profitable, especially if you examine what has happened. The more you know what you have done previously, the better you will be able to prepare for future situations.

Experience in both World Wars, civilian disasters, and other catastrophic events teaches that understanding and preparation for an event enhance the capacity to overcome fear and other stress responses. The human mind constructs thought models of future situations from personal experience as well as from information communicated by others. To the extent that your characteristic responses are very much built into your nervous system, you will respond to new stresses with characteristic responses. You can master these alarm responses and concentrate your intelligence on a practical mastery of the situation.

How you handle an anxiety-producing situation—either on the job, in the home, or in the community—will depend on your own particular temperament, constitution, and general way of handling things. You ought not resort to a mechanical formula applicable to others, but should use a method more compatible with your own particular way of life. People learn this lesson slowly. They tend to emulate others in their conduct of life, rather than master ways suited to themselves. New situations require new solutions. The more you look for your own solutions, relying on your own assessments, the stronger you will become.

Fear of losing the support of others is the basis of most fears. Even fears of heights, bridges, and crowds result from the tendency to assume that others are more concerned with you than they actually are. The same fear accounts for the tendency to tolerate unsatisfactory situations in the hope of future rewards.

You can overcome fear and other negative emotions that inhibit positive action. While constitutional factors may influence your tendency toward fear reactions, you have learned your attitudes and responses to fear and can therefore modify them by knowledge and experience. Optimism and effort ensure the success of an activity. Don't find fault with others or with situations when things go badly for you. Stop and examine the extent to which you can modify your actions and revise your expectations about difficulties. As George McDonald said, "No man ever sank under the burden of the day. It's when tomorrow's burden is added to the burden of today that the road is more than a man can bear."

You may be discouraged; you may fail to accomplish your objectives; you may conflict with others or feel inadequate, relative to them. Forget it. You don't need more ability, opportunity, resourcefulness, or other assets. But you may need to learn how to use what you have. Most times this will be sufficient to reach your goals. Do you believe it's not worth the effort? Do you say "What's the use, I'd better stick to my usual routine; I'd better do what my neighbors are doing; I'd better not stick my neck out"? If you do, you have not realized that the effort itself has force and momentum and will help you to overcome obstacles and create a reality out of what you may have only imagined.

Keep alert for situations that generate the five great enemies of peace: avarice, ambition, envy, anger, and pride. Petrarch said:

"If those enemies were to be banished, we should infallibly enjoy perpetual peace."

Avarice comes from believing that you need certain things when you probably don't, and from the feeling that what you depend on will be taken from you.

Ambition arises from dissatisfaction with yourself and your activities. It's fine to set up challenges and to want to succeed. But excessive ambition will lead you to set unattainable goals and to become too focused on the outcome. Pursue your objectives at a pace suited to your temperament. Concentrate on your efforts, not on the results. As the Caliph Ali said, "Thy lot or portion of life is seeking after thee; therefore be at rest from seeking after it."

Envy comes from an irrational comparison of what others have achieved and what you have achieved. Lack of what others possess does not cause frustration, but failure to develop your assets does. Envy erodes confidence, fosters a "what's the use?" attitude, and leads to reduce effort.

Anger can envelop you and destroy your incentive. Whenever you become angry, review what has happened. Has somebody ignored or criticized you? Should that bother you? Must you depend on others' opinions? Have you allowed others to impose their expectations on you or control your behavior?

Pride develops from a need to impress yourself and others with qualities you lack. The mature individual acknowledges his limitations, acts humbly, and tolerates differences with others. The tyrant, depending on others to support a false view of himself, stifles his own growth and fails to realize the acceptability of his flaws. Your distress will vanish when you admit your fallibility.

To prove to yourself that you can accomplish what you set your mind to do, select one daily activity that you want to modify and for one week make a conscious effort to stick to your plan. Do something you can accomplish that takes extra effort. For example, reduce your cigarette intake from thirty to twenty per day, reduce your intake of beer from three beers to one beer per day, or climb five flights of stairs per day. Keep a written record of this. As simple as these accomplishments will be, they will demonstrate to you that you can rely on yourself to do what you want to do; and they will give you the courage to try new things.

"That which grows slowly endures," according to J. G. Hulland. Take your time; keep actively engaged in your tasks. You will reach your objectives. Hardships, obstacles, and adversities may help you choose a goal and examine your strengths. Misfortune strengthens. It teaches you what you can and cannot deal with and so prepares you for future adversity. As you master negative experiences, your confidence will grow.

The situation you find yourself in is no mere accident—it results from your habits and thoughts. The seeds of future acts are planted long before each of us passes childhood. These early experiences govern our particular behavior. How you express these early attitudes will depend on the experiences you encountered throughout growth, maturation, and life, and on the extent to which you have developed a degree of self-mastery over your impulses and the inner dictates of your conscience.

It is curious that we become not what we want to become, but what we *are*. As life unfolds we are better able to actualize our true natures. Seeking a goal, you may encounter obstacles. Nevertheless, it is only through your efforts (limited by your self-concept) that you can achieve that which you were destined to achieve in the first place. Preparation for this goes on in the back of your mind, sustained by many quiet accomplishments that will gradually enable you to evolve toward what you can become.

How much you realize your potential is ultimately up to you alone, since only you can decide how much you will try to reach your goal. If you believe you can do something, you will never give up because of obstacles. If you believe you cannot do something, you will be more inclined to give up early.

If you focus your attention on environmental or situational stresses and seek to alter them, you will neglect the causative influences in your own thought and character that in fact determine what your environment will be. It may seem easier to change others, your job, or your circumstances. But unless you realize that you can change yourself—gaining control over the very causes of your life experience—you will not modify your environment one iota.

You may believe that your difficulties

have developed from your strengths, not from your weaknesses. Actually, a test of the principles will demonstrate to you that everything that happens results from the slowly evolving expression of qualities within yourself.

Every thought bears within it the seed of particular effects; results are predetermined and correspond to the undemonstrated potential inherent in all thoughts and actions. In fact, even adversity results from the persistence of negative thoughts and inhibited actions. In fact, adversity can serve as an indicator of faulty habits that you need to modify and correct.

As you begin to focus on your strengths and not your weaknesses, as you begin to try to improve upon that which comes naturally, you will begin to modify your attitudes and actions toward others. They, in turn, will modify their attitudes toward you.

Your thoughts develop into habits and your habits result in circumstances. To change the circumstances you are in, you need only change your thoughts. Your habits will change. Ultimately, your circumstances will change. If you seek to master stress, you need only examine the problem at hand, decide what you wish to accomplish, and apply yourself to the task of daily focusing your attention on the smallest increments of activity that will lead to the objective.

Your attitudes will influence your interpretation of situations. If you anticipate good results, you will keep pressing until they occur. If you expect bad results, you will not press beyond unsatisfactory or bad results.

Everything follows a certain rhythm. Everything occurs according to a certain time span. A tree does not grow overnight. Nor does an egg hatch ten minutes from the moment of conception. Summer lasts just so long. A rainfall usually lasts several hours. When it lasts longer, we are surprised and view it as unusual. We have less knowledge of the duration of many human activities. High-speed communications and transportation mechanisms have increased the rapidity of events in the modern world and have thrown off our sense of time. It is harder to judge the duration of activities that do not simply depend on the movement of the sun and the coming and going of the seasons. It is hard to judge the time needed to accomplish tasks that depend on others, especially when we do not know their priorities.

Unless these time patterns and rhythms are learned by experience, each individual has no way of judging how much more effort is involved in completing a task or reaching an objective. Faith will enable you to persist at something for as long as it takes, rather than fall prey to cynicism and a sense of the fleeting nature of time and the necessity to hurry up and finish what's at hand, in order to get on to the next task.

⫷ SELF-RELIANCE AND WEALTH

WEALTH IS, to a considerable extent, the product of a state of mind. To live well and yet to be in constant debt, or to live above your means, will not give you the freedom of thought so necessary for maximizing your accomplishments. Many people earn much money at the price of their own individuality and sense of independence. It is not so much the size of your salary that is crucial, but rather the extent to which you feel comfortable about your standard of living, so that you can take the world on your own terms. To achieve this position of being able to determine your economic destiny requires that you reduce your standard of living to a level that gives you economic independence.

From this point you can then determine ways of carving out new activities that derive from your greatest strengths.

Self-reliance and personal independence provide the most crucial ingredients for solving the problem of wealth. Personal independence leads to financial independence. The richest men in the world have invariably depended on themselves, not others, for earning their wealth. The more you recognize that you alone are responsible for your financial independence, the more you will find ways in which to earn more.

Is the purpose of wealth or accumulated capital to purchase new items at the start of every new fad? Or is it to help you to achieve your deepest dreams? Is it to be spent on obsolescent devices or status symbols, or is it to enable you to implement your thoughts in active ways in the world at large so that you can further actualize your own resources? If you use your earnings to accomplish some worthy purpose, you will find much satisfaction and increased confidence in your efforts to earn more. The more your efforts to earn are linked to efforts to accomplish some broader objective, the more each will serve the other and increase your sense of self-realization.

"He's lucky," you may say about the person who has accumulated a fortune or who earns more than you do. "I'm satisfied with what I earn," you may rationalize. And yet you may, as many do, feel you lack sufficient money to achieve your goals. Why should you accept any limitation on the amount of money you can earn in the richest country in the history of the world? Probably because you fail to understand certain principles about the acquisition of money. In his essay on wealth, Emerson said that "wealth is in applications of mind to nature; and the art of getting rich consists not in industry, much less in saving, but in a better order, in timeliness, in being at the right spot." Efforts motivated solely by monetary reward invariably lead only to frustration. To earn money, you must search for ways to increase your contribution to society. You need only assess the nature of your skills, determine where they are most in demand, and bring your efforts to bear in the situation where they produce the most good. Money will automatically follow.

Perhaps you feel guilty about earning more money, even from your own efforts. Why should you feel guilty about working harder? Perhaps because you may have set some kind of ceiling on the amount you were willing to earn. And yet, if the objective for which the money was to be earned entailed a reasonable and worthwhile objective that would be a contribution to society at large, then certainly it would be of considerable value and well worth the hardships you might encounter. Many people set financial goals and then mistakenly remain content when they achieve these goals.

The acquisition of wealth results from planned actions designed to apply existing resources. Since money is earned from effort, not from luck or chance, you must focus on small, regular, detailed steps, which can be readily controlled and which can lead to greater earnings.

Look for ways to increase your output in your present job. Establish financial goals: the amount of money you wish to earn, the amount you wish to save, and the amount you wish to have for your retirement. Record these figures on a small index card as a reminder of your financial goals. They may alert you to opportunities as they arise.

If you set financial goals far in excess of your present income, you are well advised to determine who earns that amount, how they earn it, and what steps you must take to earn an equivalent amount. Remember not to focus on the money *per se*, but on the activities that you can pursue to earn this money.

When you earn money, you will be able to measure the value of it in terms of the work accomplished. The dollar you earn will be valued by you to the extent that you have made an effort to obtain it. If you earn it lightly, you will view it lightly. If you sweat to earn it, you will value it more and thus spend it less rapidly.

You must learn to spend money, as well, to come to appreciate its value in helping you to accomplish your ends. The value of money cannot be learned from hoarding it, but only by spending it in exchange for more desirable products or for items which will increase your capacity to earn more. Money is a form of energy; you must devote as much time learning how to spend it as you devote to learning how to earn it.

Money, therefore, can become a vehicle for enhancing your self-actualization. Unless you have this objective in mind, you are not using money wisely. You may use money to keep up with the Joneses. Certainly you should enjoy the degree of luxury that you need or desire. But self-actualization does not really derive from this kind of expenditure.

Money *per se* has no value. It is only a symbol of potential exchanges for things of value. And ultimately, it is symbolic of the individual's character. How you spend your money may reveal more about you than how much you earn. How you spend your money reveals what you value and appreciate in the world. Do you spend on others? Do you avoid spending for yourself because you feel you don't deserve the fruits of your labor? Do you trust others with your money? Are you in full command of it? Are you afraid to take risks?

A dollar in the hands of a child is not equivalent to a dollar in the hands of a gambler, an accountant, a banker, an investor, or a student.

More and more, money represents time and freedom and speed, for it enables you to conquer the globe in a way never available to the Caesars of old. It may mark the difference between the education of an individual or the freedom of a housewife. Tell me how you spend your money, who signs the checks, and I will tell you about your interests and values and the characteristic conflicts you are likely to encounter.

People often fail to recognize that money has no intellect. What happens to it depends on your values. Unless you know what you are doing with it, you may soon lose it. There is a great need to understand how you share it or use it to lord over others. If you learn the uses of money, you will learn more about yourself and about the opportunities available in the world. If you spend money in ways that will increase your ability to contribute to society, your income will increase.

A practical key to economy is to spend your money, as well as time and effort, on whatever enhances your talents. As long as you do this, you will be building your strength and will spend wisely.

The acquisition of certain expenses that interfere with more important objectives can be vexatious to the spirit and can distract you from your true aims. As the expenditure of money increases, opportunities for diversionary activities increase. These may distract you from the efforts that first proved so personally rewarding.

Spend in relationship to your own self-realization and according to some kind of plan of action. As long as you maintain a balance of your expenses in relation to your income, you are in good shape. If you keep your expenses down, you can do what you want to do. The vision of a fancy estate for your old age, if it causes you to skimp now in the areas in which you have special talents, is a mistake of the greatest order. Spend now if you wish to maximize your achievement. To save all for a vague future may deter the fullest expression of your talents.

It is society's need for certain services that determines the amount earned. Efforts in some activities may not result in the same monetary rewards as efforts in other activities. Do not begrudge others the money they have earned, which results not from luck but from the nature of their work and how they have accomplished it. It makes more sense to learn from what they do and then to decide whether one wishes to pursue a similar activity in a similar way.

Remember that you probably want more than you need, but that you are likely to settle for less than you could earn.

To summarize, spend for self-actualization and increased mastery, not just for pleasure; invest your earnings in increments that add up to a whole greater than the sum of its parts; spend to increase income rather than expenses.

SELF-RELIANCE AND DEPENDENCY

SELF-RELIANCE COMES from two separate acts: a positive orientation towards goals and a reduction of unnecessary and inhibiting dependency patterns.

Trying to meet the expectations of others in order to be accepted by them creates a compulsion to act in certain ways, which limits your own ability to fully express yourself. This is dependency. Talking at length about your plans and goals can diminish your motivation. Sharing your plans with others also creates pressure for you to meet their expectations and makes it more difficult to change your mind. Talking about your plans invites opinions that may inhibit you from taking action. Even when others respond positively to your plans, you still have reduced responsibility for your behavior. By making it a shared act, you have reduced the risk of criticism, should you fail. However, you have also reduced the sense of satisfaction you would receive from succeeding.

It's foolish to ask someone who is in one business about your chances of success in another business. The chance of accomplishment has less to do with the state of the economy than with your willingness to work toward your objectives.

Avoid commitments beyond your means or capacity; these foster dependency, uncertainty, and perfectionism. Similarly, avoid the tendency to intentionally achieve less than you can, thereby avoiding the assumption of responsibility. There are numerous delays and difficulties in modern life that provide ready excuses for such avoidance. It is easy to blame transportation tie-ups and telephone-line breakdowns when you fail to keep your appointments. If you can't attend or participate or dont want to, say so outright. Don't make excuses.

Very likely you have characteristic ways of doing things, some of which produce problems for you. You can modify these faulty action patterns. You may be meticulous, cautious, and conservative, which may help you in some instances and may prevent you from acting in other instances. Often you must make choices or decisions without all the information available to you, even at the risk of error, rejection, reprisal, or criticism. Perfectionistic trends present themselves as an excessive concentration on detail, procrastination, and indecision. Too many tasks may also prevent you from finding time to do what you want to do.

You may be so cautious and fearful of failure or criticism that you consider all alternatives before acting, attempt to avoid criticism by checking things out with others, and never complete anything so that you won't be judged a failure. You can learn to observe your own behavior patterns to see how different ones trigger different responses in others. If you can identify these patterns, you have an opportunity to modify your own behavior, maximizing your control over yourself and the indirect influences you may have on others.

Suspiciousness also results from dependency and placing too much importance on what others think about you. Many people, at one time or another, become oversensitive to the nonverbal, and often unconscious, attitudes of criticism, hostility, or rejection of others. If you find yourself reacting to real or imagined slights, don't argue with people over your impressions. It is unimportant if an occasional person has hostile or negative feelings toward you. Everyone can't like everyone else. Even if people are prejudiced against you because of your race, creed, or color, that's their misfortune. As long as they don't do anything directly to harm you, you will be better off making a conscious effort to restrain yourself from trying to challenge them or to control or influence them to change their attitudes. Accusing others of ambivalent feelings or lack of interest in you may frustrate you, foster conflict, and may provoke the very response which you anticipate. Avoid any inclination to respond to sarcasm or innuendo. Acknowledge that everyone has a right to think for himself and close the discussion. Maintaining a positive attitude will, in the long run, draw positive responses from others.

You can change such patterns of dependent behavior through action that will enable you to see factors that trigger the habit and through the development of alternative patterns of behavior. You can't change the habit if you aren't in a situation which calls it into play. Developing alternative habits may not be sufficient. Often, the new habit becomes as much of a compulsive pattern as the old. You may search for advice, exercises, diets, or formulas, only to find that such solutions can come to dominate you and distract you from your objectives.

You must deal not so much with the habit and the compulsion as with the factors in your present environment that reinforce the compulsive process. Focus on your attitudes towards other people. Are you too concerned about what they think of you? Does your perfectionism mask an underlying depression? Are you afraid of criticism? Do you focus on goals beyond your capacity? If these patterns sound familiar, you ought to take stock and define goals more compatible with your interests, needs, and skills. To do this, you may have to risk criticism, and even the anger of others. But only by acting in this independent way, learning to say no to the demands of others and yourself, will you develop confidence.

Ask yourself, "What factors in my life are draining me? To what extent am I neglecting my own needs?" Are you known as someone with strong shoulders, willing to assume all kinds of burdens? Are you known as someone who is easy to approach, so that friends, relatives, and others feel no hesitancy about imposing on your time. Positive gratification from this must be weighed against the negative price you pay in giving up free choice. Don't worry about refusing requests that seem to be demanding of yourself. It is better over the long haul for families and friends to know that what you do for them you do willingly—because you want to, and not because you hadn't enough courage to say no or enough faith in them to believe that they would support you, whatever your reasons for not helping.

Assuming responsibility that rightfully belongs to others is not unselfish behavior. When you take over a job that someone else ought to do, you are either showing them that they are really unreliable or that you can do it better; or, worse still, that you are kinder and more solicitous of them than they are of you. You have done what they should have done. No wonder you don't believe their expressions of gratitude and feel angry with yourself and those you have "helped."

Don't assume responsibility for the behavior or attitudes of others. Nor must you have all the answers. Don't try to control the feelings of your children or your spouse toward you by compromising yourself. Don't continually modify your own behavior so that others respond more favorably. Failure to recognize life's critical moments, frustrations, and failures causes this pampering of others.

It is not good for others, in any case, to have you assume the total responsibility for their behavior. A child, for example, learns as important a lesson when you say no as when you say yes. William Boetcker said, "The man who is worthy of being a leader of men will never complain about the stupidity of his helpers, the ingratitude of mankind, or the inappreciation of the public. They are all a part of the great game of life. To meet them and overcome them and not to go down before them in disgust, discouragement or defeat, that is the final proof of power."

Develop a recreational interest that absorbs your attention and efforts. Techniques of relaxation, passivity, withdrawal, prayer, and exercise reduce the unpleasant mental concepts associated with anxiety, they reduce tension, and they can renew vigor and enthusiasm. These techniques can help control self-defeating and impulsive reactions to anxiety, which may lead to excesses such as those associated with overeating, alcohol abuse, and drug abuse.

The ability to withdraw into solitude will increase your faith in your capacity to achieve your objectives. It will also give you strength to endure frustrations and uncertainty. Time spent alone thinking about your goals and the steps you are taking to reach them will give a larger purpose or meaning to your efforts and will revitalize confidence, particularly when you are plagued by persistent distressing thoughts of your problems. Woodrow Wilson said we grow great by dreams. "All big men are dreamers. They see things in the soft haze of a spring day or in the red fire of a long winter's evening. Some of us let these great dreams die but others nourish and protect them, nurse them through bad days 'til they bring them to the sunshine and light' which comes always to those who sincerely hope that their dreams will come true."

Unfortunately, spending time alone with one's own thoughts creates anxiety for many people and accounts for much escapist activity. Learn to listen to your own thoughts. This will help you to learn more about your inner self and your real goals. Spend some time alone each day familiarizing yourself with your thoughts. You can do this while walking outdoors or relaxing at home, in a church or synagogue, or even in the public library. This solitude will provide you with an opportunity to clarify and to become comfortable with your feelings and thoughts and to assess the strategies for reaching your objectives.

The ability to withdraw into such solitude in the presence of others will also prove an invaluable skill in various crisis and conflict situations. At times of stress or pressure, withdraw into a quiet corner to examine your thoughts. Don't feel obligated to act immediately. This ability to contemplate and evaluate situations in terms of your broader objectives will give you the strength and sustenance to cope with problems far greater than those you usually must handle.

Learn to "keep cool." Delaying your responses to others will reduce the urgency that magnifies the significance of events. Suspend judgment until you can assess a situation calmly in the light of your limitations and strengths. Delay will enable you to stand outside of tense situations, to assess priorities, and to decrease your vulnerability. To the extent that you control your life, your involvement in relationships and activities when they occur will be genuine and free of fear. Delay does not mean postponement. It simply means control over snap judgments. Make decisions when you are away from a situation and can think alone. In time, you may be able to do this in the presence of others.

THERE IS a direct link between service to others and rewards in life. Whatever you put into effort will result in reward. You need not give much consideration to the nature of these rewards or to whether or not you will obtain them, for they will appear to the extent that you concentrate on making the most of your efforts. Nowhere will this be more apparent than in your relationships with people.

Along these lines, Confucius wrote that "he who wishes to secure the good of others, has already secured his own." This means that the benefits you derive from the world will be in direct proportion to the benefits that you provide to others. This relates both to individuals and to the public good.

Who can you serve? Where can you make a contribution? Look at the people around you, your family, friends, coworkers, customers, and others whom you meet in daily life. To the degree to which you provide or contribute to the welfare of all these people, you will be rewarded.

We live at a time in history when the world is fast becoming a global village. Nations are dependent on other nations. Communities relate with other communities. No one can be an island unto himself. It is impossible to live in any community without in some way providing some kind of service to some groups of people, just as it's impossible to live in a community without receiving the services of other people. The more you recognize this interdependence, the more you will want to make an active effort to cooperate with others.

Relationships are strongest when they develop in pursuit of a shared objective or activity. Relationships that focus on simply "having a relationship" will prove taxing, frustrating, and generally much less rewarding. Where differences exist in attitude, values, and objectives, do not try to modify the other person to suit your needs. Similarly, don't allow yourself to be so accommodating that you compromise your own identity. Find shared interests and activities and pursue these. Accentuate the positive features of a relationship; conflict and recrimination will subside.

Don't dominate or tyrannize others. The more you can define your particular skill and interest area, the more you can differentiate what you can contribute to a particular situation and what others can contribute. Not all activities involve cooperative effort. Many complex processes can be divided into discrete activities that one person can do alone.

The contribution of autonomous individuals working together on those individual tasks that they do best alone makes for the strength that comes from cooperative effort.

John Galsworthy said: "The essential characteristics of the gentleman were the ability to put himself in the place of others, the horror of forcing others into positions from which he himself would recoil, and the power to do what he feels to be right without considering what others may say or think."

Imposing obligations on others to do certain things demonstrates fear, not strength. Strength comes from the ability to do what you want to do yourself. Examine all those situations in which you are telling others what to do without regard for their capacity to determine their own direction. Stop and listen to others. Recognize that they, too, have special individual needs. You can help them if you allow them to pursue ththeir own directions, not if you impose fixed expectations that you think are best. Listening to others will help you to understand what they want and how you can cooperate with them to improve your relationships with them.

Remember what William James wrote: "The first thing to learn in intercourse with others is non-interference with their own particular ways of being happy, provided that those ways are not assumed to interfere by violence with ours." Accept others as they are. Don't expect that they are going to modify themselves to meet your expectations.

Are you ignoring your children or your parents because of some peculiar set of priorities that puts business associates or potential clients over and above those who are most important to you? Are you really being honest with the business associates or are you kowtowing to them? Are you doing what you expect they want of you rather than what you want to do? Do you see this as a more important priority? If so, face up to it and don't overindulge your family to absolve your guilt. Be honest, and they will accept you as you are.

When you have difficulties with others, search for alternative ways of relating. Consider this even if the other person is over-emotional, hostile, and vindictive. Examine how you detoured from your original course. Have you been discouraged by unrealistic envy of the assets or achievements of others? Continual comparison of yourself with others will invariably distract your attention from your own objectives; rarely, if ever, will it produce any positive benefits, no matter how much you may rationalize about the value of measuring yourself against others.

Remember what Emerson wrote: "There is a time in every man's education when he arrives at the conviction that envy is ignorance; that imitation is suicide; that he must take himself for better or for worse as his portion; that though the wide universe is full of good, no kernel of nourishing corn can come to him but through his toil bestowed on that part of ground which is given to him to till. The power which resides in him is new in nature, and none but he knows what that is which he can do, nor does he know until he has tried. Not for nothing one face, one character, one fact, makes much impression on him and another none."

Have you been sidetracked from your objectives by a competitive drive or social pressure to compete? This can dilute your efforts from activities in the area of the strengths, interests, and resources that will ensure success. Competition for prestige in areas where you lack competence may also create a sense of inadequacy.

It is amazing what a change in attitude can do for improving relationship. You can prove this to yourself in the following way. For one week, make a conscious effort to find one area of mutual interest with everyone you meet for the first time. For one week, make a conscious attempt to listen to the whole story of those who seek your advice. Do nothing more. Don't give your advice, opinions, directions, or criticism. Allow yourself one week to think over what you yourself can do that will help others to help themselves. What is there that you can praise about their performance or attitude? What broader perspective can you suggest to them, which will add an element of hope to their misfortune or excitement to what now bores them? What suggestions can you offer that will enable them to maximize their own resources in order to accomplish their objectives?

As simple as this sounds, you will no doubt find it hard to do, for it is hard to resist the temptation to sound like an expert or to delay response when others urgently demand solutions. It is hard to keep quiet when you believe you have the answers to someone else's problem.

What, then, is to be gained by this week of delay? If in the week's delay you consider the special and unique qualities of others, you will come to realize that the solution to their problems can really only come from their particular strengths and their style in approaching problems. Your own experiences in the same situation are less likely to prove applicable to them than their own previous experiences in dealing with similar situations. Ultimately, they can only do it their way; the best you can do is to recognize that fact and perhaps to help them to see that as well.

If you wish others to respect you, you must show respect for them. For twenty days, approach everyone you meet, irrespective of his station in life, as if he or she were the most important person in the world. Everyone wants to feel that he counts for something and is important to someone. Invariably, people will give their love, respect, and attention to the person who fills that need. Consideration for others generally reflects faith in self and faith in others.

For the next twenty days, act towards others as you would want them to act towards you. Treat others as they want to be treated. Approach each day as if you were the most successful person in the whole world. This attitude will readily become a major bulwark against petty irritations and misfortune. Faith in yourself and in others will help you to keep your head when you encounter daredevils on the highway or when problems are dumped on your desk. Faith in yourself and in the world around you will enable you to overlook the foibles of mankind; you will pursue your course rather than slip into an attitude of frustration and anger.

Remember that association with others

does not mean that you have to define yourself in terms of membership in a clique or group. Prejudice derives from people's eagerness to be accepted by a group of like-minded people who provide mutual support by excluding others. The creation of an "outgroup" automatically defines the "in-group." Become your own "in-group." As Washington Irving wrote, "There is a healthful heartiness about real dignity that never dreads contact and communion with others, however humble."

How often have you refused to associate with someone because you found him stupid or ignorant, or because you didn't agree with him? How often have you ridiculed, criticized, or scorned others because they were of a lower station or had less education than you? Don't be afraid to associate with people whom your neighbors may consider "ne'er do wells" or "foreigners." How many of your friends are just like you—of the same school, with the same education, of the same religion, the same economic group, and so forth? I'm not sure you can learn very much that way. You can learn much more by recognizing that there is something to be learned from everybody. Each of us has a story to tell and a unique perspective of the world. The way to understand the world is to see it from as many viewpoints as possible.

You don't have to accept other views, but openness to ideas will help in the discovery of your own viewpoint. As you clarify your own views, your interest in the perceptions of others will increase. Recognize the limitations of your own perspective. Others have their own truths, which are just as valid for them. Theodore Roosevelt said: "There is a point, of course, where a man must take the isolated peak and break with all his associates for clear principle; but until that time comes he must work, if he would be of use, with men as they are. As long as the good in them over-balances the evil, let him work with them for the best that can be obtained."

Until you can leave a group without fear of being rejected, you will be under pressure to conform. How can you reduce this pressure? Focus on your goals, reduce communicacation overload, avoid preoccupation with the past and future, avoid envy of the activities or achievement of others, and avoid competition. Possessiveness, jealousy, unreasonable demands, and neurotic obligations to conform to the expectations of others must also be avoided.

Rousseau wrote: "Take the course opposite to custom, you will almost always do well." Consciously avoid conforming to the social group at the expense of your uniqueness. Ignorance of the limitations set by others, coupled with time spent alone, nourishes imagination and achievement potential. If you take your lead from others, you will be frustrated and increasingly dependent on them and will limit your achievement. No doubt, you derive much satisfaction from your activities with others. But participation in groups should suit your interests and your time schedule and come from genuine desire, not a sense of obligation.

The search for happiness and a life free of problems will bring less satisfaction to you than involvement in productive activity. A permanent state of comfort is incompatible with existence. Efforts to achieve it are likely to fail. Maximum involvement in present activity dispels egotism, false pride, petty jealousy, and wasteful competitiveness, and brings real satisfaction.

According to John Foster, one of the strongest characteristics of genius is "the power of lighting its own fire." Those who accomplish much have a unifying purpose to their life and express themselves in whatever manner, shape, or form that is necessary to achieve their purpose. Call it simplicity, humility, or self-sufficiency. You may believe that a Stravinsky, an Einstein, or a Picasso has, by his genius, earned the right to be eccentric, idiosyncratic, self-willed. I contend that the decisions to become masters of their own fate gave them the courage to try new things. The willingness to think the unthinkable requires courage to spend time alone, to run the risk of ridicule. Not everyone is a Picasso, but everyone can consciously distinguish himself from the world around him.

Set aside time to pursue your own objectives. This will give you the strength and capacity to express your uniqueness. Light your own fire. Pursue your own objectives without fear of failure, censure, or criticism. This will free that unique combination of factors that lie buried beneath your social self. Many of your conflicts may very well be due to the suppression of this inner self. To the extent that you can discover your inner self, you will be able to bypass many of the numerous conflicting expectations that are imposed upon you by the complexities of modern society. The more you follow a fixed course, the more you will be able to become that which you are capable of becoming. You shouldn't have to modify or accommodate yourself to each new situation. It's easier to be yourself wherever you are. Where conformity governs you, you will be continually shifting from situation to situation.

Set limits in your personal relationships. At work, avoid those involvements that distract you from your job. Avoid ill-defined helping situations that engender feelings of exploitation. If concern about the responses of others hampers your self-expression, don't seek out leadership or managerial roles. Find situations in which you can comfortably assert yourself without worrying about negative feedback from others. You can change your mind more readily if you have said no instead of yes. If you have difficulty saying no and tend to overcommit yourself, don't make decisions hastily. Take your time to think things through.

No one can get along without some kinds of assumptions about the nature of the world. In the broadest sense, a philosophy of life or a religion provides this perspective. It is a framework of expectations about life and rationalizations about misfortune that are handed down from parent to child in the form of spoken and unspoken traditions and prejudices. These expectations are only slowly modified as the individual tests his mettle against the realities of the world. In a sense, this is what anthropologists refer to as culture, the commonly shared perceptions, beliefs, and attitudes about the nature of the world.

·✦ CONCLUSIONS

EVERYONE FEELS inadequate from time to time. Some even feel inadequate all of the time. Feelings of inadequacy are generated by a comparison of oneself to others, not failure to accomplish a task.

When you feel inadequate, stop for a minute and consider what you do have. Do you have your health? Do you have friends? Do you have free time? There will always be something positive in what you do have. Ultimately, satisfaction will come from those activities you pursue from the position you are in now.

Reaching an objective may not satisfy you for long. As such, you must seek new objectives to pursue. Satisfaction comes from the process and the attainment of the goal, not possession of it. Of course, acquisitions will make you feel good. But the feelings won't last. Your mind needs new activity.

Your mental activity is as much a part of you as your heartbeat and respiratory rhythm. Your life is neither the activity outside yourself nor the organization you belong to, and you can't really define yourself accordingly.

You will find peace of mind when you determine and act in terms of your own nature and in terms of your goals. Greater understanding of the power your thoughts have in influencing your state of being and becoming will bring you much satisfaction. This understanding will result also in a greater appreciation of the differences between you and others who have their own characteristic thoughts and attitudes.

Lastly, you will find satisfaction when you stop trying to affect the results of things directly and concentrate only on causes on that you can use to accomplish your dream.

A sense of humor can also provide perspective and the capacity to differentiate yourself from the situation in which you find yourself. You may also gain the objectivity through prayer or physical activity. Develop one such technique to use when pessimism or a negative frame of mind occurs. Shift to it before you have made serious mistakes in handling a problem. Swift said: "Although men are accused of not knowing their own weakness, yet perhaps few know their own strength. It is in men, as in soils, where sometimes there is a vein of gold which the owner knows not of." The time you are wasting thinking about your inadequacy could be spent searching for that vein of gold in your activities and yourself.

---❧ DAILY CHECKLIST

1. Work to improve that which you do best and most readily. As much as possible, rely on yourself to accomplish the goals you have set for yourself.

2. Concentrate first on activities related to the objectives that are most important to you. Much can be accomplished in a short time if you devote yourself to your highest priorities. Keep track of time expended in activities so that you can better monitor your daily routines. Don't succumb to the feeling that you have insufficient time to do what you want. If you focus on your major objectives, you will minimize or halt those activities that have no real importance. You will

be increasingly free of the pressure to pursue less important activities.

3. Prepare a general schedule the night before, but approach each day in a relaxed way, letting things emerge and evolve as the day goes on. Above all, seek activities that you enjoy. When you finish one activity, move on to another.

4. Focused and informed activity reduces fear and anxiety. Study of a task and the actual effort of testing it lead to knowledge. Remembering this will take the sting out of failure, which, in fact, should be a source of new information that can assist you when you can return to the task. Criticism, however unpleasant, can provide valuable information about ways to improve. Make the most of the information and resources you now have, and don't dwell on potential sources of difficulty that are beyond the lim-

ited amount of information available to you. This will only magnify illusions of fear and anxiety. Postponement can become habitual and can lead to nonproductivity. Don't procrastinate by fantasizing about past failures or future problems; don't allow yourself to be distracted by opportunities for self-indulgence. When you postpone an activity, you increase the chances of never accomplishing it, and you will be left, in the future, with memories of past wishes rather than of past deeds.

5. How you handle an anxiety-producing situation—either on the job, in the home, or in the community—will depend on your own particular temperament, constitution, previous training, and experience. Don't resort to mechanical formulas to solve problems. Find the method most compatible with your own personality and life style. You can learn from emulating others, but you should

strive to conduct your life in ways suited to yourself. New situations require new solutions. The more you look for your own solutions to new and problematic situations, the more likely you will find the best approach for you. Don't blame your inaction on others and take credit for sacrificing your goals on their behalf. This demeans them and creates insecurity about your "true feelings."

6. Acting in terms of your goals will give you strength in dealing with the most complex situations and will minimize the psychological threats of specific situations. Ultimately, what you accomplish results from your willingness to be true to yourself. Stick to what you find most rewarding. This will make your life more rewarding and will minimize your conflicts.

7. The strongest relationships develop from pursuit of a common objective or activity.

This shared experience increases tolerance for differences in attitudes and values and reduces efforts to try to change others for the sake of the relationship. Relationships that focus on simply "having a relationship," as such, can prove taxing and frustrating. Similarly, guard against a willingness to be so accommodating that you compromise your own identity.